CLAUDE

CLAUDE

RANDY MORAVEC

G. P. PUTNAM'S SONS

NEW YORK

G. P. Putnam's Sons

Publishers Since 1838

200 Madison Avenue

New York, NY 10016

Published simultaneously in Canada

Library of Congress Cataloging-in-Publication Data

Moravec, Randy.

    Claude / by Randy Moravec.

        p.   cm.

    ISBN 0-399-13792-0 (alk. paper)

    1. Cats — Anecdotes.   2. Cats — Pictorial works.

3. Moravec, Randy.   I. Title.

SF445.5.M678   1992   92-15596

636.8 — dc20   CIP

Printed in the United States of America

1   2   3   4   5   6   7   8   9   10

To my parents, who taught me
that having a pet is a big
responsibility

Claude was one of a steady stream of strays who found their way to my brother's house on the edge of a small agricultural town. It was there that we met. He seemed to like the company of humans. Feeling softhearted, I took him home. That was ten years ago.

One morning, while I was removing Claude's fur from a shirt, it occurred to me to calculate how much fur Claude shed in a day. As a point of idle interest, I calculated the amount he shed over a month, a year, and finally over his anticipated life span of fifteen years. This piece of statistical feline trivia proved to be a hit at social events, and I decided to keep a closer eye on Claude so that I could record other socially relevant statistics.

Claude proved to be a willing assistant in this task — the additional attention and tidbits of food he received provided sufficient motivation to help. His dedication to the project extended to spending time in the darkroom, and more than one print had the benefit of an actual cat hair or two.

C L A U D E

Claude and I collected data without the burden (or benefit) of exacting scientific method, and we have embellished the statistics whenever possible, so your results may vary. The sample base for our statistics was not large in number (one underachieving indoor cat). However, most of the statistics are based on repeated trials and tests over a period of time.

Claude and I would like to thank Turk and Sally for giving Claude his first break; Dorothy Spencer of Read/Write Press, who now can say "I told you so," for convincing me that Claude was adorable; Hillary Cige, Anna Jardine, and The Putnam Berkley Group for their support; and Suzanne West for her design skill, photographic critiques, and endless copywriting contributions. Without all of them, this book would not have been possible.

CLAUDE

ESTIMATED NUMBER OF CATS

CURRENTLY POPULATING THE

PLANET:

240,000,000

(144,000 MILES PLACED TAIL

TO NOSE, OR MORE THAN

HALFWAY TO THE MOON)

With the number of cats inhabiting the planet today, it may be difficult for humans to understand why cats have not organized. A voting population of 80 million cats in the United States, after all, would have a profound lobbying impact on Washington, yet cats remain a loosely knit group of underachieving mammals. This probably is due to a lack of ambition (if Claude is any measure). After all, if you were provided with a roof over your head, abundant water and food, unqualified affection, and medical care, in exchange for making a pleasing sound or appealing gesture once or twice a day, how ambitious would you be? Humans work hard for thirty or forty years to enjoy an equivalent lifestyle for the last twelve to eighteen years of their lives — about the typical life span of a cat.

C L A U D E

TOTAL IMPACT FORCE OF

LANDINGS ACCUMULATED

BY A CAT DURING

ITS LIFE:

547,501.01 POUNDS PER

SQUARE INCH

38,583.58 KILOGRAMS PER

SQUARE CENTIMETER

The accumulated impact force of landings is approximately that of thirty pounds of TNT — enough power to propel a typical sedan for sixty-odd miles or light your house for a week. With the force expressed in these terms, one can see the possible usefulness of a cat as a power source. Claude, for example, makes a resounding *thump* when he lands, generating potential energy. It is tempting to harness this power so that he works for his keep. This, however, would interfere with his primary function (although research has yet to determine what it is).

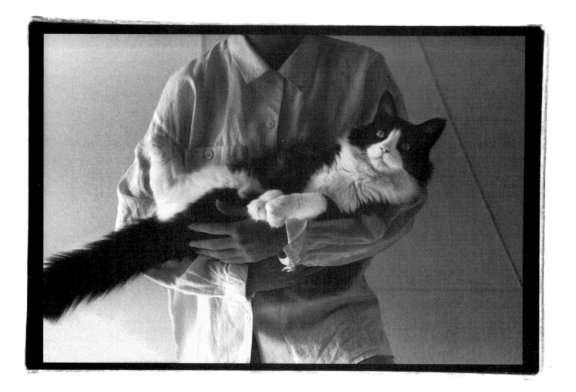

C L A U D E

At first it may seem amazing that a creature so unresponsive to names can accumulate such an impressive collection of nicknames. Nicknames, however, occur for that very reason. Our research has shown that there are several distinct categories:

Generic baby-talk names: These are used not only for cats, but for anything about the same size as a human baby. They are delivered in a high-pitched voice reserved especially for this purpose. Claude, for example, is often called "Baby" and "Kitty" (despite his advanced age), as well as "Botsy-boo" and "Bitsy-waa."

Behavior-related names: Often a cat's behavior elicits a specific nick-name. Claude's impressive collection of these names includes "Lump," "Rodent," "Slug," "Piggy," and "Oinker."

CLAUDE

Suffix-addition names: In this style, the cat's name is used as a root word to which suffixes are added. Claude is often addressed as "Clauddles" or "Claudie." Suffixes also are added to nicknames — Claude sometimes is called "Sluggo" or "Lumpy."

Rhyming names: This type of nickname often features suffix additions. The style of rhyming depends on the cat's basic name and current nickname. Claude, for instance, has been addressed as "Claudie-Waddie" and "Oinker-Boinker."

Change-of-possession names: These are not for addressing a cat directly, but for talking about it (generally when the cat is present). A change-of-possession name generally reflects the cat's most recent activity. After performing a new trick or striking an endearing pose, Claude becomes "my cat," whereas after a trouble-seeking or shedding activity he becomes "your cat." When a series of particularly annoying activities has taken place, total dispossession may occur—Claude becomes "that cat."

C L A U D E

TOTAL AMOUNT OF HAIR

A CAT SHEDS DURING

ITS LIFE:

14,904,000.00 HAIRS

14.95 POUNDS

6.78 KILOGRAMS

(661.58 MILES END TO END)

Shedding rates vary among cats — these figures are based on Claude, an American longhair. Short-haired cats may shed more profusely to compensate for their hair length.

Not only does it seem that cats can shed copious amounts of hair at will, but also it appears that they can select the color of the hair so that it contrasts with the surface they shed on. Claude, for example, has the uncanny ability to shed black hair on a white dress shirt and white hair on a black suit. He can do this simultaneously, often without making direct contact. He tends to prefer shedding on surfaces that are expensive or difficult to clean. Some humans look upon shedding as a cat's form of revenge.

CLAUDE

Do you know why lion trainers use a chair? It is not to fend off potential attacks from the felines they are training, as is commonly thought, but to have a comfortable place to sit while trying to get a cat to do something other than what it would prefer to do.

Claude, being an exceptionally food-oriented cat, has learned a great variety of tricks. (In true Pavlovian tradition, all of them are associated with food.) Many cats, however, consider the mere consumption of food tricky enough. Their owners seem to agree, for they go to great lengths and expense to have this simple trick performed.

C L A U D E

When it comes to obeying a command, a cat is the equivalent of a two-year-old human — only an emphatic "No" gains any attention. It seems odd that a semi-intelligent creature such as a cat would be unable to heed a simple command. Our research has indicated, however, that cats respond to the volume and pitch of a voice rather than to particular words — it is not what you say but how you say it. Calling "Claude" in a normal voice, for example, elicits absolutely no response, whereas a loud shout or a high-pitched stream of gibberish produces instant (if unpredictable) results.

It is only fair to note that we humans respond to cats at the same primitive level. We often ignore the soft *meow* issued to remind us that feeding time is near. However, an authoritative *MEOW* sends a clear message to us that food is overdue, and we respond accordingly.

CLAUDE

From an aerodynamic point of view, cats are not designed for flight. Claude's drag coefficient, for example, has been calculated to lie somewhere between that of a poorly formed brick and that of a furry shotput. Despite this design flaw, Claude can be seen hurling himself through the air several times a day.

Every year, thousands of cats leap from buildings that are four, ten, and even twenty stories high, in the misguided notion that they are creatures of flight. Most survive the experience, although some of them require mending that can run into expenses rivaling those of bypass surgery. Perhaps all this flight is due to a misunderstanding — cats may have overheard humans talking about the advantages of compiling frequent flying (freak went flying) miles.

CLAUDE

TOTAL ALTITUDE A CAT

ACCUMULATES DURING

ITS LIFE:

202,027.50 VERTICAL FEET

38.26 VERTICAL MILES

61.57 VERTICAL KILOMETERS

If a cat attained its total lifetime altitude all at once, it would be in the part of the atmosphere called the mesosphere — the altitude at which meteors vaporize.

Please note that this statistic is based on an average indoor environment — outdoor cats have higher altitudes available. However, when food and fragile objects are situated in high places within an indoor environment, the total altitude of an indoor cat can double. When high places are expressly off-limits to cats, the figure can triple. If a cat attained these higher altitudes all at once, it could reach low earth orbit. This would place it within shedding range of many spy satellites.

C L A U D E

TOTAL TIME A CAT SPENDS

GETTING INTO TROUBLE

DURING ITS LIFE:

14,968.26 HOURS

623.68 DAYS

1.71 YEARS

Next to eating, getting into trouble seems to be a cat's favorite activity. Even the most tolerant cat fancier may be driven to mild hysteria when his or her cat unstuffs a handmade Italian leather sofa or lunges toward a shelf of heirloom crystal.

Claude's repertoire of troublemaking activities includes reorganizing carefully arranged stacks of papers, turning on a keyboard just before walking on the keys, and redistributing the contents of the garbage disposal. Most of these activities are timed to happen at irregular intervals between midnight and dawn. He excels at making noises that can be heard but not deciphered by humans until they are fully and reluctantly awake.

CLAUDE

Curiously, a cat's behavior can strongly resemble a dog's when it comes to food (although you seldom will hear a dog or cat owner admit this). Claude's food-related attention span, in cat terms, is very nearly indefinite. When his attention is focused on food, he often gives the impression of a truly devoted pet while he tolerates expressions of human affection such as petting, scratching, and hugging.

CLAUDE

Attracting and holding a cat's attention with something other than food is often futile. For example, Claude's attention span can be so brief that, for all intents and purposes, it cannot be measured. However, our research indicates that another factor also influences attention span: there appears to be a direct and inverse relationship between the cost of an object and the length of time a cat pays attention to it. A five-dollar wind-up mouse, for example, warrants virtually no attention, whereas a scrap of paper found in a neglected corner will keep the cat fascinated for minutes.

We humans find this trait particularly puzzling because our higher level of intelligence informs us that expense and fascination go hand in hand.

C L A U D E

TOTAL AMOUNT OF APPROVED

FOOD A CAT CONSUMES

DURING ITS LIFE:

6,335.33 OUNCES

395.96 POUNDS

179.60 KILOGRAMS

A cat consumes the equivalent of a good-sized cow in its life-time, which probably is more than the combined weights of its owners. For humans, this is the equivalent of consuming an average brontosaurus.

Please note that this statistic represents only the approved food consumed by cats. It does not include unapproved foods that are obtained by begging and performing, nocturnal scavenging, or plate and bowl licking, or the nocturnal consumption of nonfood items such as flowers. This is because unapproved items consumed by cats generally are returned to their owners as inexpressibly revolting morning surprises.

C L A U D E

TOTAL AMOUNT OF

UNAPPROVED FOOD

A CAT CONSUMES

DURING ITS LIFE:

2,857.51 OUNCES

178.59 POUNDS

81.01 KILOGRAMS

Unapproved food is anything a cat consumes without permission, including cat food that is obtained in an unapproved way. Claude's unapproved food list includes an astounding array of items, ranging from broccoli, crackers, cantaloupe, and kiwi fruit to sticky plastic toys, extension cord insulation, dried branches, and the heads of flowers (his favorite is baby's breath). It must be noted, however, that Claude's branch-chewing and cord-munching activities often are merely indirect ways to obtain approved food — he tends to pursue these activities only around dawn, in order to announce that it is time to eat.

C L A U D E

TOTAL WEIGHT OF THINGS

CAUGHT BY A CAT DURING

ITS LIFE:

3,840.85 OUNCES

240.05 POUNDS

108.88 KILOGRAMS

A British study shows that the average well-fed outdoor cat brings in about sixteen pounds of game a year, ranging from mice and rats to bullfrogs and voles. These unfortunate victims rarely are consumed by the cat; rather, they are presented proudly and conscientiously to their owners as a sort of rent payment. Although many owners may find this practice somewhat disgusting, it should be kept in mind that this is probably the closest thing to work that a cat will ever do.

Being an indoor cat, Claude has limited prey available. He would need to catch fifty or sixty good-sized spiders to equal even one mouse. To maintain his statistics and to keep in practice, however, he occasionally catches a bypasser's arm or leg.

C L A U D E

For many cats, a yawn is a signal that the animal is tired or bored. For some cats, a yawn is a means for displaying a formidable oral cavity. For Claude, yawning also is an exercise that helps keep his mouth and jaw muscles in top form for his favorite activity, eating. Each cat develops a unique style of yawning. Claude often vocalizes when he yawns, emitting a noise usually associated with heavy machinery that is operating improperly.

C L A U D E

TOTAL NUMBER OF TIMES

A CAT VOCALIZES DURING

ITS LIFE:

246,375

Although cats can hear sounds far outside the range of human hearing, they focus on emitting sounds well within human range. Cats have several ways of producing sounds in order to communicate. Claude, for example, can make sounds with his voice box, his purr box, and several combinations of the two (depending on what he wants to communicate). He also can make himself heard by using props — usually any fragile object in the house — and he can perform both solo and quartet recitals on the piano (fanfare for humans and four paws).

CLAUDE

For cats, "awake" and "alert" are relative terms — although cats often appear to be awake, they only occasionally appear to be alert. For instance, Claude's awake state would be considered light sleep in humans, whereas his alert state often includes behavior that would require institutionalization for humans. Our research has indicated that Claude spends eighty percent of his day sleeping, eight percent of his day dozing (barely awake), three percent of his day trying to stay awake, and three percent of his day trying to get to sleep. This leaves six percent of his day for actual alert activity, most of which occurs during the night.

C L A U D E

TOTAL TIME A CAT

SLEEPS DURING

ITS LIFE:

74,982.75 HOURS

3,124.28 DAYS

8.56 YEARS

Scientists report that cats sleep away much of their lives because of a predatory instinct to conserve energy for the hunt. Hunting, however, is a learned skill for cats. Indoor cats such as Claude either have received inadequate training or have neglected their hunting skills because food is plentiful and within easy reach. Nevertheless, their instinct for excessive sleep remains. After consuming a large portion of food in the briefest possible amount of time, cats are overwhelmed by the urge to sleep. In humans, this pattern usually is associated with the middle-aged sports fan.

CLAUDE

TOTAL TIME A CAT REMAINS

MOTIONLESS DURING

ITS LIFE:

7,256.25 HOURS

302.34 DAYS

0.83 YEARS

Claude's eating and sleeping abilities are matched only by his ability to remain virtually motionless for long periods of time. Neither awake nor asleep, Claude stares blankly out a window or at a wall, unresponsive to external stimuli such as humans.

Our research, which indicates that these periods of motionlessness tend to follow the consumption of food, has led us to formulate the steady-stare theory. This theory states that after a meal, all available blood rushes to Claude's stomach for digestion, leaving little or no blood in reserve for brain functions. This produces an even deeper semiconscious state than is usual for a cat.

C L A U D E

TOTAL TIME A CAT SPENDS

LOOKING UP DURING

ITS LIFE:

16,425.11 HOURS

684.38 DAYS

1.88 YEARS

It is a wonder that cats do not suffer constantly from neck cramps as a result of spending so much time looking up at their owners to figure out what they are doing. (It also is remarkable that cat owners do not suffer from similar neck cramps looking back at their cats.) It certainly would be advantageous to be able to look one's pet straight in the eye, which is probably why people keep their bird cages at eye level, but the relationship between cats and humans would change considerably if cats were large enough to look at their owners eye to eye.

C L A U D E

TOTAL DISTANCE A CAT

IS TRANSPORTED DURING

ITS LIFE:

197,100.12 FEET

37.33 MILES

60.08 KILOMETERS

Most cats are equipped with four strong legs. These can propel them to speeds that exceed twenty miles per hour, or break a fall that would cause serious damage to a human leg. Despite this, we have a tendency to relieve a cat of all ambulatory responsibilities. Claude is relieved of these responsibilities on a regular basis. Although there is no direct human parallel, consider the following scenario: Your car suddenly rushes up to you, honks its horn several times at octaves far above normal range, scoops you up, carries you around at random, and then drops you off in no particular place.

CLAUDE

There have been many heartwarming stories over the years about cats who traveled great distances to be reunited with their beloved owners, but the average housecat's powers of navigation and self-sufficiency are frighteningly slim, as many cat owners will tell you. Claude, for example, can take no more than a few steps of a journey into the great outdoors without being distracted off course by a leaf, ant, rock, or twig.

Uncharmed by the urban wild and unimpressed by travel, Claude prefers to lounge on the television and wait for things to come to him. On a good day, Claude may travel up to 150 yards (not including human-assisted transport).

CLAUDE

Cats are good at hiding — they can disappear for minutes, hours, and even days. When humans cannot see a cat at first glance, they tend to assume the worst: The cat is in imminent danger and must be saved; it is devising a new and insidious way of getting into trouble; or it will be lost forever unless a search begins immediately. Fortunately, Claude chooses his hiding places on the theory that if he cannot see you, you will not be able to see him. When he discovers that you can see him, the hiding place no longer serves a useful purpose (except as a depository for fur or an ambush point). His favorite hiding places are drawers (and behind open drawers), closets (particularly those with dry-cleaned clothes in them), and boxes of all sizes and shapes.

CLAUDE

Most cats consider the idea of getting wet an unpleasant experience that is akin to being on a medieval torture rack. Claude is no exception. He forever seeks ways to avoid being bathed — little does he know that one of his favorite napping spots was designed expressly for washing. Although he would be in favor of streamlining the washing process so that it would take as little time as possible, he probably would prefer the standard sink to any of the automated devices around the house.

Claude tolerates washing because the flood of sympathy that follows his ordeal is accompanied by generous offerings of treats.

CLAUDE

A cat purrs at a rate of about sixty cycles per second. This is comparable to the typical rate of a "million fingers" bed massage, and it seems that both have similar effects on people.

The cat's purr may be one of the few attributes that led to its domestication. Cattle and goats were domesticated for milk and meat, horses for transportation and labor, and dogs for protection and hunting. With all of these helpful creatures gathered around primitive man, it is a wonder that cats were domesticated at all. The cat didn't do much, was poor eating, and preferred to hunt alone. On the other hand, it was soft, furry, and emitted a pleasing purr, so the cat was tolerated for its aesthetic value and became the lava lamp of its day.

C L A U D E

A commonly overlooked benefit of a cat is its ability to act as a passive (very passive) solar collector. Claude, for example, possesses all of the attributes needed for the collection of solar energy: he is dark, he has a large and ever-expanding heat collection area, and he is mobile (occasionally) and dense (usually). These attributes make the cat a far more efficient solar collector than asphalt or granite, although cats remain well below those most efficient of all solar collectors, black car seats.

*British thermal units, also known as big tabby units.